At the Noisy Café

Joe Dolce

Selected Poems 2017 - 2023

First published by Busybird Publishing 2023

Copyright © 2023 Joe Dolce

ISBN: 978-1-922954-32-9

This book is copyright. Apart from any fair dealing for the purposes of study, research, criticism, review, or as otherwise permitted under the Copyright Act, no part may be reproduced by any process without written permission. Enquiries should be made through the publisher.

This is a work of fiction – and even that ain't true. Any similarities between places and characters are… well… similar! So what.

Cover image: 'Joe/Newspaper' and back cover painting, 'Blue Mythology' by Lin van Hek.

Cover design: Busybird Publishing

Layout and typesetting: Busybird Publishing

Busybird Publishing
2/118 Para Road
Montmorency, Victoria
Australia 3094
www.busybird.com.au

Dedication

Les Murray dedicated his books to the Glory of God
but, as he's already used that one, this book is dedicated to
Lin van Hek
(which is, more or less, the same thing)
for my literary re-awakening
and a forty-three year love affair.

Go for it, Joe!
for Joe Dolce

Go for it, Joe!—do what you have to—
criticize—clarify—and always
with love—the young burn each other
at the stake—rampant

around conflagration—
but we're the old guys now—
the nation doesn't need more fire—
why rake up spent coals?

showed Gebhardt who remarked "I like that—*with* love—
i'm rereading Auden who said the same"—a thought arises:
imagine coming home to Auden—the Auden who *came home* …
conceive "home" as one does "poem"—

answer the adversaries for the love of poetry, Joe—
like Kinsella urged the other day—
signature windmill of speech & gesture—
"i've got nothing at all against any geezer—

it's only ever about poetry"—
(*in medias res*)—
i've warmed to enemies as though long ago's
flames—bless 'em—bless 'em, Joe!

~ **Kris Hemensley** ~

Contents

And Let the Wonder In

Hælþ blétsung	2
St Corona	3
Le grand masked ball of phantasmagoric Melbourne	4
Unfathomable	6
Aliens	7
And let the wonder in	8
Carmenta'lia	10
Song of Nestor	11
Short poem	14
Saint Ælfgifu	15
Photographing black wallabies	16
Frozen kittens	17
A toast to free verse	18
Mowing the fields of Elysium	19
Season of fire	20
Vase	22
Brown snake crossover	23
Royal night out	24
Kero aphrodesia	25
Painting	26
Doppelgänger	27
Car with the lot	28
Stepdaughter	29
Gall revisited	31
The sound of one shear clicking	32
Horsewitch	33

Brokenheart

Broad Arrow Café	36
The murder of Alberta King	37
Last meals (dead man eating)	38
The tyger	40
Daddy plus one	41

Our loss	42
Brokenheart	44
Fairweather's garden	45
Enitharmon's bower	46
Miss Ohio dummy	48
Shoemaker's moon	48
Kissing grandma	50
Chả ốc	52
The ballad of true and false singing	53
Aloysius' lament	54
Empty strollers	55
The ballad of William Crowe	56
In repose	58

Don Diego's Accordion

Don Diego's accordion	60
Gluten-free toast	61
Clearly not Fourth Street	62
Constellation	64
Starvation box blues	65
Gingerbread house	66
Fracture	67
I said left, at the fork, Robert - *Left!*	68
Topophilia with Leunig at Officeworks	69
Dumb phones	71
Catoptromancy	72
Wolf	73
Rubik's paradelle	74
Muse-wrestling	75

The Cavafy Villanelles

Prost	78
I never found those lips again	79
Roll-your-own Lamb	80
Bach blind	81
Knife penny	83
Barbarians	84
Homage to Shead	85

Yubitsume	86
Vitis vinifera	87
Korean triptych	88
Narcissus shaving in the river	89
The Cavafy Villanelles	90
1. Fifty-nine retired	90
2. Hericleia	91
3. At the noisy café	92
4. Days of 1926	93
5. Bath	94
6. Literati	95
7. Ithaca	96
8. Almost mythical	97
9. Nyktoporia 1932	98
10. Last embrace of Alexandria	99
And ever shall be	100
author's statement	102
special acknowledgments	104
publication history	105
about the author	106

And Let the Wonder In

Hælþ blétsung

May thee be whole, uninjured, of good omen,
in helthe, sanative, free of ague, caducity, malison,
cleansed, bedward, exempt from crookback,
flux, glabriety and gyve.
Neither vexed by halt, or immedicable,
infrequented by leech, nithing, peeler, picaroon,
brabble, quidnunc, scapegrace and varlet.
Abundant in snyttrucræft and treowthe.

Translation:

Health blessing

May thee be whole, uninjured, of good omen,
in health, healed; free of fever, senility, curse,
cleansed, rested, exempt from hunchback,
dysentery, greasiness and fetter.
Neither vexed by limp, or incurable wound,
unfrequented by doctors, cowards, police, pirates,
squabbles, busybodies, rascals and knaves.
Abundant in wisdom, loyalty, truth and kindness.

St Corona

Latin for Crown.
Patron saint of plagues.
Testified for a Roman soldier,
named Victor, a Christian,
whipped by the Christian-hating judge, Sebastian,
during the reign of Marcus Aurelius,
eyes gouged out, yet
refused to deny Christ.
Corona, sixteen,
wife of a soldier,
knelt and prayed for Victor.
Imprisoned, tortured,
drawn and quartered,
in 177 A.D, Syria.
Pre-congregation saint,
her feast day, May 14th.
St Corona's bones were exhumed,
in 1943, and found to be
both male and female.

Le grand masked ball of phantasmagoric Melbourne

Why no! It's but a mask, a lying ornament.   Baudelaire

Passersby, welcome!
To the rough music of charivaris,
the spectacle of the fragmented crowd,
New Victorian Gothic,
where Dior and St Vincent de Paul
social-distance, in frantic masquerade,
strolling under the eaves of the Orangerie,
down Rue Danse Macabre.

But oh! What elegant company!
Like opposing magnetic poles,
how we veer away from each other,
Poe in Red Masque,
Baudelaire in Black,
(who appraised black clothing
as the quintessential sign of modernity).
ZOOM with Shakespeare and Lear,
come now, in general equality,
to watch Beatrice dance with Benedick,
in *Much Ado About Twitter*,
SCREAM with Munch,
(recall that he painted it, while infected),
and over there, in the eve,
the quarantined Boccaccio
scribbling *l'Umana commedia*.

Les Medames et Messieurs!
Let us emerge now from the abbey,
with hidden faces, altered personalities,
both concealing and revealing secret expressions.
Come to *Une Fête Galante*!
Au Bal Masqué!
Follow *La fée Verte Virale*
into the hall of mirrors,
trailing lilac, spider net and tassel.
Lipstick not essential,
only kohl and a half-niqab.

Onward to the Mardi Gras of *Memento Mori* -
'remembering that we must die' -
Kings and Queens! Doges!
Dukes and Duchesses!
Marquises and Marchionesses!
Déguisez moi, chic follies,
with rich handkerchiefs of Guipure lace,
star of pearls, white kid gloves and shoes.
Aux Clowns de La République!
Le Beau Monde!

Unfathomable

The gills started growing
in the eighth year of lockdown.
The shuttle had brought back
a strain of virus so virulent,
nothing could stop it.
I think our bodies knew the spores
couldn't survive in seawater
and so began reconstructing us
to survive.

It has been ten years
beneath the waves
and what remains of the race
has adapted remarkably.
Our skin is now green-brown
and a clear translucent film
covers eyes, and, of course,
webbing between toes and fingers.

The majority of us
live in communities,
mainly for protection,
and to abate loneliness.
My family and I prefer
to live apart, deeper down,
where it's cooler,
and less hectic.

Occasionally, we holiday
to the surface, letting the sun
remind us of our youth,
floating briefly, under the warmth,
gazing at the edge of land mass
off in the distance,
as unfathomable to our grandchildren,
as the sea once was to us.

Aliens

The aliens have grown together
years in the small container
have caused them to turn to each other
in their yearning

fine silky white roots
braid together they drink
as one feed as one but
are two distinct creatures

if one should fail before the other
the other may survive
but if you try to separate them
too roughly both
will surely die

sometimes gentle shaking
can free lives like this
roots release their grip
delicate white nerves
suddenly pulling loose

when we were torn apart
I said time to die now
one might say I've mostly recovered
but often in the dark
the scar aches
where our skins joined

when I breathed deeply inside you
and you slept wrapped all around me
and we were but one creature.

And let the wonder in

a choral libretto in eight movements

1. It is part of the Cure to wish to be Cured. *Seneca 9 BC*

2. Dr Edward Livingston Trudeau was sent, as a young man, to the mountains, where he expected to die of consumption. But he did not die. As he lay in bed, he had a vision of a great hospital where he could rebuild other sufferers. Flat on his back, he examined patients not as ill as himself. He raised money, and laboured, until his dream became the great Sanatorium at Saranac. *Louis Bisch*

3. Sometimes the more measurable drives out the most important. *Rene Dubois*

4. Healing must involve a change in consciousness, as well as a change in somatic symptoms. Something unconscious, or forgotten, must be recalled, or something be allowed to sink into forgetfulness. *Ralph Twentyman*

5. The witch doctor succeeds for the same reason all the rest of us succeed. Every patient carries his own doctor inside him. They come to us, not knowing that truth. We are at our best when we give the doctor, who resides within each patient, a chance to go to work. *Dr. Albert Schweitzer*

6. After laughter, all the muscles are relaxed, including the heart; the pulse rate and blood pressure temporarily decline. Muscle relaxation and anxiety cannot exist together and the relaxation response, after a good laugh, has measured as lasting forty-five minutes. *Dr. Bernie Siegel*

7. When you stand at someone's side, nourishment may be provided that can carry that person forward, for a week or two. During that time, anything can happen. *Norman Cousins*

8. The young woman speaks: Will my mouth always be like this? she asks. Yes, I say, it will because the nerve was cut. She nods and is silent. But the young man smiles. I like it, he says. It's kind of cute. All at once I know who he is. I understand, and I lower my gaze. One is not bold in an encounter with a god. Unmindful, he bends to kiss her crooked mouth, and I - so close - I can see how he twists his own lips, to accommodate to hers, to show her that their kiss still works. I remember that the gods appeared in ancient Greece, as mortals, and I hold my breath, and let the wonder in. *Dr. Richard Selzer*

Carmenta'lia

The frass on the mimosa indicate
larvae have tunnelled the stem,
weakening it so that seed is impossible.
Drawn out by pheromones,
the nymphs unfold transparent wings.

O foe of fruit tree and timber,
how far you have flown
from your Roman namesake,
Carmenta, goddess of childbirth,
patron of midwives,
your praises once sung
by Ovid, Servius and Solinus.

Song of Nestor

In the time of strife and sorrow,
in Salonika, lived Nestor -
student of Saint Demetrios,
the Myrr-Streamer- with purest love
for Christ, his faithful Ancestor,
between the burning time of Rome,
by Nero, and the Edict of
Milan, where Christians found safe home,
under kind Constantine the Great,
Caesar was Christ's enemy - hate,

murder and persecution fell,
from Maximianus's hand,
on those who would testify, tell,
of the Sovereignty of Christ
over Caesar's privileged command,
and though Roman syncretism,
for most pagan beliefs, sufficed,
there could be no criticism,
or disloyalty to the State,
or One God before Caesar's gate.

This Emperor persecuted
Christians, in blood-thirsted games,
on a custom stage, reputed
to be built on pillars, with spears
points upward, in bordering frames,
to pierce the bodies of the slaves,
thrown to their deaths, amidst loud cheers,
by Caesar's favourite depraved
Vandal, the strong-boned and ruthless
goliath, known as Lyaeus.

Each afternoon, Lyaeus slew,
for the amusement of the crowd,
Christians; by wrestling, threw
them onto the forest of spears,
to writhe and suffer, prayers aloud
for the Saviour to break their Chain,
beseeching our Lord Christ to hear,
and grant Heaven's Cloud, free from pain.
Nestor, seeing this, and heart-torn,
challenged Lyaeus to come forth,

but first sought St Demetrios -
condemned to perish in prison -
for blessings; a Sign of the Cross.
The sage prophesied to Nestor,
in a weak and whispered voice, 'Son,
you will overcome Lyaeus,
but, for our Christ, you must suffer.'
Fortified by God, and armed, thus,
he went to meet the giant's rage
in battle, on the killing stage.

Maximianus, in pity,
offered Nestor reprieve from death:
'Your youthful dare and fantasy,
is admired, your courage, whim,
that you might win, acquire wealth –
but I would dissuade you with gifts.
My Lyaeus - do not fight him!
You won't prevail, I urge: desist
from your challenge, sheath sword and knife,
take my gifts: keep your youthful life.'

Nestor heard these things but feared not
the strength of Lyaeus and spoke:
'I am not here to fight for naught;
neither for gain, nor for my pride,
but to make your cruel beast choke
on his own blood; to defeat him,
in the name of Christians who died-
to bring God's Judgment for his sin.'
In anger, the Emperor rose:
'Then let us end this idle boast!'

Nestor crossed himself: 'Lord help me.
Demitrios, give me courage!'
Striking Lyaeus, at his knee,
the goliath fell to the floor,
and, with God's strength, he choked the Scourge,
wrestling him onto the spears,
where the heavy giant was gored,
discovering death held him near,
the people shouted, in loud throes,
'Great, the God of Demetrios!'

But Maximiamus, well-shamed
before the throng, and in sorrow
for his lost Champion, now blamed
Nestor, ordered him beheaded
by his own sword – a single blow.
So met our Lord a brave pilgrim,
beside Demetrios wedded
in death, reborn in Christ's Kingdom.
Released, by God's good Grace, from strife,
St Nestor quit this earthly life.

Short poem

Verbophobia: fear of words.
Hippopotomonstrosesquipedaliophobia: fear of long words.

Saint Ælfgifu

for Dr Houston Dunleavy

If a blind man or a deaf worship at her tomb,
they are restored to health and prove the saint's merits.
He who went there lame comes home firm of step,
the madman returns sane, rich in good sense.
                    -William of Malmesbury (1125)

Queen Consort, *Concubina regis*,
in 939, first wife of King Edmund the Magnificent,
(who was murdered by Leofa, the thief,
while attending mass in Pucklechurch).
Mother of two future kings,
Eadwig, and St Edgar the Peaceable,
(the latter's daughter, St Edith of Wilton,
regalis adelpha, conceived from an affair,
with a religious woman of noble birth,
whom Edgar stole from a nunnery -
although bride abduction was traditional,
Edgar did penance, by not wearing his crown seven years.)
St Ælfgifu's name joined Old English
elements of *elf* and *gift*, (she frequently gave
her expensive clothing to the poor).
Refounded the Royal Nunnery of Shaftesbury,
(a house connected with her mother, Wynflæd, a Vowess)
where her body is buried and enshrined.

Common ancestor to both Queen Elizabeth II,
and Diana Spencer, Princess of Wales.

Photographing black wallabies

By the time I raised the lens, they had gone,
the black wallabies on the track today,
I missed the photograph – except this one.

Careening to right and left, coming down
the hill, in front of the car, and away,
by the time I raised the lens, they had gone.

They darted along the edges of brown,
like circles, in the fluid of sight, play,
I missed the photograph – except this one.

The sky was pink, the sun had spun down -
coming to drink at the low waterway -
by the time I raised the lens, they had gone.

A rufous orange stained the wide chest of one,
except the tip of its tail, which was grey,
I missed the photograph – except this one.

So swiftly, through the high ferns, they were drawn,
to the water, heads low and tails out straight,
by the time I raised the lens, they had gone,
I missed the photograph – except this one.

Frozen kittens

They're not staying in the house!
My mother, fearful of ammonia
urine-sprayed carpets of spinster aunts,
so three Twiggy-eyed kittens,
go out into the pink garage.
My carpenter dad builds a wooden hut
with a hole-door, opening onto
a papered half-cardboard box.
I feed them milk, table scraps,
mashed spaghetti, canned fishy catfood.

That weekend, four feet of snow forces
my father awake to light the coal,
at dawn, shovelling a white corridor
to the pink garage.

I carry my saucer of warm milk,
push my hand into the dark cathole,
feeling the cold hard things.
I pull my fingers back, as though frostbit,
without looking, turn,
hurry back through the snow tunnel,
to the warm kitchen,
again uncertain of the universe,
praying for school.

A toast to free verse

While I appreciate rhyme,
the elegant end of a line,
where syllables chime
to pleasing effect in the mind,

there is still much to be said,
for the words that won't go to bed
with every cheap vowel that winks,
whistles, whispers or clinks.

So a toast to the line
that refuses to rhyme

like this one.

Mowing the fields of Elysium

Brilliant Buddha gold
alchemy of yellow & white, the soul-
colour of triumph, from Calf to Ring,
the Mean, the Ratio, the Rule,
the truest lode said to rest at earth's core,
now blowing here in two-metre-high dry grass.

Aeneas and I toss a Bough on the Arched Door,
pull-start the Red Rover Regal 4-stroke hand push,
three tugs to turn it over,
wheels raised to Highest Setting,
into the Great Rush of Whirling,
blades threshing, carats, leaves, flakes, dust,
catcher-catching the coinage, straw-scattering
aurum shining dawn, ausum glowing dawn,
the swarming 40 degree smoulder.

Homer said, of the Elysian plain,
no snow is there, nor heavy storm, nor ever rain.
The sun is murder.
I pause, sun struck in Fleece,
my bucket-hat soaked,
then, indoors for relief,
cold water in a blue claw-footed bath.
The Esky of the Afterlife
yields an ice-cold XXXX Gold.
A few minutes lie down,
by the waters of Okeanos,
near Aeolus's rattling pedestal fan,
then back to work.

It's said these bright plains border
nearby Lethe, the River of Forgetfulness,
between the Clifts of Tedium and Apathy,
this narrow square of the Blessed and Happy,
our unbaled bush Champs-Élysées.

Season of fire

after CJ Dennis', A song of rain, 1915

Because of heated atmospherics
on the Tasman Sea,
or hot air from the Never Never
reaching Toolangi,
or Brolga's broken emu egg,
whose yolk burst into flames,
a million acres of bushland,
by bushfire is defamed.

Roar on roar on Rubicon,
through the Thompson & Acheron,
cinders sparks and ash bad luck,
for Tanjil Valley and Matlock,
Friday thirteenth so unkind,
in nineteen hundred and thirty-nine,
melting tire, melting wire,
a hundred and fourteen degree fire,
for the winds are ever turning
and it's burning . . . burning . . . burning.

Because three pressure systems
joined to drive the wind,
because of prolonged drought,
the land was dry as sin,
or soaring cinder turning
daytime into night,
black smoke blinding even
accuracy of sight.

The exploding gums of Warrandyte,
the scorch of Cudgewa and Bright,
the suffering leaves of Curryong,
the burning birds of Narbethong,
all flutter, fire, ash and gone,
along the Yiri lines of song,
Sun Mother in the Dreamtime weeps,
her tears evaporate in heat,
for the clouds are ever turning
and it's burning . . . burning . . . burning.

Vase

Charred French hunting horn,
hooking a stump,
roofing tin twisted by Brâncuşi,
glass heat-fused to plates,
crockery powdered to mosaic,
handleless garden tools.
Every inside now an outside.

Standing in the ruins of the home,
raking through rubble,
looking for a whole anything,
the house which held many objects of memory,
now itself a memory,
memories consumed by memory.

A hand-made stone chimney stands,
towering unsteadily, punch-drunk,
still on its feet, although no one can see how,
its gape-mouthed gargoyle hearth,
splintered and battered.
Why do chimneys survive bush fires?
Is it quiet understanding between
the small ritual fire place –
our human offering -
and the great devouring Fire God,
some recognition of kin?

Remnants of a river stone painted by a granddaughter
we haven't seen in six years.
Half a pottery head thrown by a son
who no longer speaks to us,

and a handful-sized round vase,
its O-mouth of wonderment,
sitting undamaged in the epicentre.

Brown snake crossover

Waltzing the track,
I catch my balance, back-
stepping with a Whoa!
as the lustre rope shimmies, slow-
ly S-bending into bush,
before I can blink,
            slink-
ing off, our pas-de-deux
                    kaput.

Royal night out

Under Augustan protection,
of absolute darkness,
bare-arsed rain
once again cavorts,
drunk and uninhibited.

Hours later, hungover,
and embarrassed,
after a long night's revelry,

naked raindrops quickly
slip out of wet garments,
for Victorian dawn.

Kero aphrodesia

Last night Lin woke me from a deep sleep
with a tick on her back
holding the flashlight in my teeth
I began with a burnt match
but only burnt Lin causing her to curse
then kerosene which also did little
finally she yelled *just pull it off*
so I grabbed it with my fingernails
and yanked it out I hope
it didn't leave any pincers in there
back in darkness the kero made it hard
to sleep so we made love instead
I love the smell of kero in the midnight.

Painting

She has spread canvas across
the long side of the shed,
and sits on a low stool, washing blue
over white weave.

She likes plein air, the humid day
cut by breeze, sitting close to the blue,
peripheral vision boxed by blue.

This first coat, the primer,
a blue sky, streaked with promise
of nimbus, bird, visitations,
is still empty, awaiting the dream state.

She works the weave,
each day adding, and subtracting,
layering, scraping, applying colour.

The waking, unannounced,
adheres to no timetable, chronology,
calendar or deadline; line upon line,
share upon shape, until closed eyes

snap open, brush lowered,
the work completed (if a work is ever completed),
the sleep, the coma, the alpha state dissipating,
the dream now alive, and breathing
there, outside herself.

Doppelgänger

In sheer pink cotton dress,
you lower yourself
into the still pool.

A *Rorschach doppelgänger*
rises seamlessly up.

Car with the lot

for Minh Nham

Two decades, since stepping
into an automobile cattle yard,
felt uncomfortable, but necessary,
to replace our hoon-stolen 4Runner.
People are always saying I resemble Kim Jong-un.
The Toyota business manager looked Korean.
You'll find Peacocks, Seagulls, Pigeons,
Magpies and Quail out here.
Peacocks are management, with puffed up strut.
He gestured outwardly.
Seagulls are yardmen, eyeing
new customers, like chips.
I'm a Pigeon. I relay information.
Magpies circle the Second-hand.
Quail are Service.

On his desk, a neat array
of Salesman-of-the-Year trophies,
handles-on-hips.
I see you got Gold this year, I commended.
What's next? Platinum?

No. Retirement.
Big Kim Jong-un smile.
But you're still young, I said.
Yes, I know, he cooed.

Stepdaughter

for Sara van Hecke

You are daughter,
yet not daughter.
The old language was stepdaughter
but there is no step between us.

My hands moved
through your hair
as a girl, as a woman,
now you've asked me
to take it all off,
before the chemicals
can do it.

Facing away from me,
your open neck exposed,
my bright scissors cut
away years, falling to the floor.

An electric shaver leaves
furry cap and finally,
my hands full of warm lather,
a whispering razor's edge.
You're newborn,
except for the now revealed
remnant cicatrix from childhood,
when you smashed through
the car's front windscreen,
before seat belts.

I towel you off,
hand you hand-mirror,
you regard yourself stoically,
but still manage some laughter.

Now you are looking at me,
with all the surrender of the world.

You are daughter,
yet not daughter.
The old language was stepdaughter
but there is no step between us

Gall revisited

The GP put down his pen.
-You've got stones,
a small cyst in your liver,
not cancer,
but I'd like to read the report.
Maybe a CT scan.

While sitting there, my thoughts
filling with tumours,
the telephone interrupted:
 - Well, put him in an ambulance
and send him to the hospital. Now!
He's eighty-five years old,
in final stages of renal failure -
the sole carer of his wife,
who has dementia -
so put her in the ambulance, too.

He hung up, turned to me,
with a dissociative look,
as if to say, Now, where were we?
I smiled.
 - Compared to that I guess I'm blessed.
 - Good, he said.
I'll see you on Thursday.

The sound of one shear clicking

The young woman in the rear
of the Ninh Hiệp fabric market stall
trimmed her fingernails
with oversized silk scissors.
I extended my own hand playfully,
indicating she might do mine, too.
Instead, she pointed the blades down,
in the vicinity of my crotch area, clicking once.
Older Vietnamese women around us laughed.
Hell, I laughed too.

Horsewitch

Fan I begood my craft they passed me neth the horse's belly,
An' ower his back, an' tween his legs an' oot aneth his taillie.
William Christie

The first Horseman was said to have been Cain
Xenophon 300 BCE stressed operant conditioning for vicious
intractable behaviour due to abuse or accidental trauma
horse whispering known simply as natural horsemanship
abused animals like abused children trust no one expect the worst
reassurance over punishment premise that teaching through pain and fear
does not result in best outcome rather patience leadership compassion firmness
The Society of the Horseman's Word
eighteenth century Scottish secret society trade union
horse trainers blacksmiths ploughmen
magical rituals to provide abilities to control both horses and women
with a single Horseman's *wird*
horsemen with powers called Horsewitches
descended from pagan cults once persecuted in witch trials
the whisperers' secret phrase of power: *sic iubeo* – 'thus I command'
a Horsewitches' two fetishes
the milt –fibrous matter from the tongue of a colt still
in its mare's womb swallowed when born
old horsemen careful to extract it immediately after birth
the frog's bone – fresh killed toad left on whitethorn bush
once hard and dry buried in anthills a month
until only skeleton tossed onto full moon running stream
little crotch bone separating itself floating
against the current this bone was kept
initiation rituals reading passages from the Bible backwards
oaths gestures passwords a handshake
stench of sulphur and alarming noises heralding
the arrival of the Devil
blindfolded initiates directed to shake His hand
grasped a cold wet hoof.

Brokenheart

Broad Arrow Café

Broad Arrow Café was busy that day,
the tables were arranged tightly to heel -
two minutes of terrible shadow play.

A Colt AR-15 Carbine at bay,
Martin Bryant went in and ate a meal.
Broad Arrow Café was busy that day.

That's not funny, someone heard someone say,
not realising the shots were too real,
two minutes of terrible shadow play.

A re-enactment, or Port Arthur play?
Customers trapped, with no place to conceal,
Broad Arrow Café was busy that day.

Twenty-nine rounds fired in the café,
ten people wounded and twelve people killed,
two minutes of terrible shadow play.

Families could not comprehend the affray,
crouched in corners, they covered and kneeled.
Broad Arrow Café was busy that day,
two minutes of terrible shadow play.

The murder of Alberta King

Slain in church while she was praying,
in thought, and words, let us recall,
the murder of Alberta King.

Six years before, she felt the sting,
in Memphis, saw her poor son fall.
Slain in church, while she was praying,

the congregation heard them ring:
six shots - the killer fired them all,
and murdered sweet Alberta King.

Eyes closed, she had finished playing,
The Lord's Prayer, from her organ stall,
slain in church while she was praying,

her husband near her, worshipping,
smoke, from the pistol, left a pall
o'er the murdered Alberta King.

Marcus Chenault fired, while standing,
in nineteen-seventy-four. Recall,
slain in church while she was praying,
the murder of Alberta King.

Last meals (dead man eating)

Lawrence Russell Brewer.
(Murder. Lethal injection.)
Two chicken-fried steaks.
Half kilo of barbecued meat.
Triple-patty bacon cheeseburger.
Meat-lover's pizza. Three fajitas.
Omelette. Bowl of okra.
Half litre Blue Bell ice cream.
Peanut-butter fudge with crushed peanuts.
Three root beers.
He ate all of it. Texas stopped last meal privileges after that.

John 'Killer Clown' Gacy.
(Rape, 33 counts of murder. Lethal injection.)
Dozen fried shrimp. French fries.
Bucket of KFC - original recipe.
Gacy once managed three KFC restaurants.

James Edward Smith.
(Murder. Lethal injection.)
A lump of dirt for a voodoo ritual.
The warden refused. Smith settled for yogurt.

Thomas J. Grasso.
(Two counts of murder. Lethal injection.)
Steamed clams and mussels.
Burger King double cheeseburger. Barbecue spare ribs.
Two strawberry milkshakes. Half a pumpkin pie.
Can of SpaghettiOs.
Last words: "I did not get my SpaghettiOs.
I got spaghetti. I want the press to know that."

Victor Feguer.
(Murder. Hanging.)
A single unpitted olive.
Requested the pit be buried with him.

Ricky Ray Rector.
(Two counts of murder. Lethal injection.)
Steak. Fried chicken. Cherry Kool-Aid.
Pecan pie.
Left the pie, telling the guard, 'I'm saving it for later.'

The tyger

Tyger tyger, striped and lean,
Marsupial thylacine,
What immortal mind might think,
To make one such as you extinct?

Blame the bounties, blame the dogs,
Blame the sawn and rolling logs,
Blame disease, the human slur,
No one really knows for sure.

Some say the last one of its kin,
Went by the name of Benjamin.
No proof or records of that tale:
The photographs suggest female.

In what bush, in what brush,
In what dry Eucalyptus,
Nocturnal hunter, quiet and shy,
Hid thy graceful symmetry?

Tyger tyger, striped and lean,
Marsupial thylacine,
Did we glimpse thee on that track?
Perhaps a clone will bring you back.

Daddy plus one

for Blaise van Hecke (1968-2022)

Not my birth daughter, she was the sun,
a loss her mother can hardly bear,
she said I was her daddy plus one.

No warning, no illness, a sharp stun,
she was taken from us, so unfair,
not my birth daughter, she was the sun.

She left behind her first love, two sons,
two brothers, a sister in despair,
she said I was her daddy plus one.

We comfort each other but she's gone,
for what's broken, there is no repair,
not my birth daughter, she was the sun.

Days stagger by, my heart is so numb,
her soft photographs are everywhere,
she said I was her daddy plus one.

No one can replace her, there is none,
how can we live without her sweet care?
Not my birth daughter, she was the sun,
she said I was her daddy plus one.

Our loss

for Blaise van Hecke

The 2 am call to me from her husband, the dread of telling her mother the horrific news, the anxious drive to the Austin Hospital, still half-asleep, the long wait in the hospital parking lot with her sons and their partners (COVID rules), her mother finally allowed in, with the husband, the rest of us much later, watching her quietly lying on the hospital gurney, on a ventilator, unsure what to do, the necessary drive back home to await the brain specialist, the CT scan, the numbing drive back to the hospital, the gathering in the waiting room with her older sister, her older brother (whom we haven't spoken to in seven years, the embrace and emotional reconciliation), the crushing news that it was hopeless to operate (catastrophic brain bleed), the decision to turn off the machines, the nurse reading through organ donation forms, a final farewell to her and heartbreak of listening to her mother whispering close to her, as though she could hear, how much she loved her, the leaving her behind, the silent drive home, the knowledge life-support was turned off, the reality of loss hitting us over the next days, her mother, in the bath, weeping that she couldn't go on, the desperate embraces at night, the intermittent and interrupted sleeps, the planning of the funeral, at first, no idea how to proceed, the service to be held at Montsalvat Colony, the choosing of the cardboard coffin (her wish), the idea for her youngest son to paint it, his trepidation that he wasn't able (too much grief), his grandmother's encouragement and offer to work beside him, adding flowers, the unforeseen dental emergency requiring her to have antibiotics and rest, the decision to let her grandson complete the painting alone, his brilliant achievement, the drive to Montsalvat to inspect the venue, the preparations: catering, printed programs, live video feed, photographic slideshow, order of eulogies and social media invitations, the late morning drive on the day for the ceremony, her husband's uncertainty whether anyone would come, the hall filling with an endless stream of family and friends, the gaily painted coffin covered in freshly-cut flowers, the moving service, her sister, husband and two sons speaking through their weeping, the fine measured talk by the esteemed author (a last minute addition), the reading of May Swenson's *The Key to Everything*, her mother's wonderful stories and memories with her, her oldest son's wife's unexpected but memorable recitation from the daughter's final book, *The Road to Tralfamadore is Bathed in River Water*, the wheeling of the coffin out into the sunny courtyard, the guests writing short messages on the box, the utterly perfect day, the furious bellbirds chiming, her coffin stripped of flowers carried to the hearse and driven away, the tea, cut sandwiches and scones in the long hall, the emotional goodbyes, the long slow drive, back home, exhausted, the days upon days following with intermittent tears and joyful recollections, of the lost daughter, that never end.

Brokenheart

Singing in her song she died. Tennyson

Takosubo cardiomyopathy.
Brokenheart Syndrome.
Not blockage.
Heart stunned by adrenaline.
Left ventricle balloons out.
Named for resemblance to Japanese octopus-trap.

Chest pains, shortness of breath,
often mistaken for attack.
Death rare. Reversible.
Almost exclusive domain of women, at 90% -
Little Ann, in *Where the Ferns Grow*,
Lady Montague, in *Romeo and Juliet*,
Padme, in *Star Wars*.
Recently, Debbie Reynolds.
Men aren't immune. King Lear.
Johnny Cash, four months after June.
Long-term companions follow each other,
often within weeks, sometimes hours.
Triggered by unexpected loss,
(including financial), fierce argument,
domestic violence, detection of cancer,
legal problems, natural disaster,
public speaking.

Fairweather's garden

after Gethsemane, by Ian Fairweather

Four years prisoner-of-World-War-I camps,
captured by Germans, in France, (his parents
left him a toddler, returning for him,
a ten-year old), peeking from cubism,
climbing bamboo barbs of calligraphy,
depression often his black prayer, he knelt
in Darwin, in abandoned boats and trucks,
escaped crucifixion, on the rough raft
he built, sailing to Indonesia.
They thought he was lost, but he saved himself,
and died, was buried, on the third day rose,
lived, 'till he was eighty-two, on Bribie.

Enitharmon's bower

for Catherine Blake

i.   Innocence

Adorn'd she was indeed, and lovely to attract thy love, not thy subjection.
Milton, Paradise Lost

He said then I love you... and I was his,
x on our wedding vow, illiterate in this world,
I understood him in the other.
He taught me as though a child.
Soon I was cutting plates.
We engraved each other's souls.
I illuminated his broken heart.
Our love held forty-five years.

ii.   Experience

So dear I love him, that with him, all deaths I could endure, without him, live no life.
Milton, Paradise Lost

He called me his shadow of delight.
I handled the money and was barren.
We prayed to our Lord
for a Swedenborgian surrogate,
consulted Judges, on concubines;
Clement of Alexandria, as to whether
wives should be held in common.
I turned away no William...
stay Kate. I will draw your portrait...
then his hands lost purchase on the tools.

iii. Innocence regained
What hath night to do with sleep?
    Milton, Paradise Lost

Each marker a stone tongue,
a vast conversation plot of soul.
Rows of granite books, resting on bones.
I run my fingers along grooved
edges of sympathy and remembrance,
the chisel-cut small space allowed us
in the Dissenter's Burial Ground.
Open mausoleum of stars above, I long
for my own stone voice to shout
heaven, speak fluently the last language.
Mr Blake is patiently teaching me.
Word-by-word, illuminating my suffering,
as if he were in the next room.
Soon, I will have a bright volume to give him.
He knows I am coming.
It will not be long

Miss Ohio dummy

Mackenzie Bart, 22, and her
ventriloquist doll, Roxy,
won Miss Ohio 2014,
with a rendition of Mary Poppins'
Supercalifragilisticexpialidocious.

My nineteen-year old cousin,
Barbara Joyce Randa,
won Miss Ohio, 1954.
I remember, at seven years old,
sitting on her lap, dumbstruck,
whispering that I loved her.
She made me promise to wait,
until I grew up,
so I could marry her.

She broke my promise.

Shoemaker's moon

And, when he shall die
Take him and cut him out in little stars
And he will make the face of heaven so fine
That all the world will be in love with night
And pay no worship to the garish sun.
> *Shakespeare*, Romeo & Juliet

He'd trained as an astronaut for the moon,
disqualified by a doctor's report,
there on the surface, his ashes were strewn.

From Addison's Curse, he wasn't immune,
he'd tracked eight hundred asteroids: his art,
and trained as an astronaut for the moon.

He died in Australia, much too soon,
exploring a crater, his life cut short,
there on the surface, his ashes were strewn.

Eugene Shoemaker, that cold afternoon,
was left alone in the regolith dirt,
he'd trained as an astronaut for the moon.

Luna Prospector carried the tomb
of Shoemaker's remains, on the transport,
there on the surface, his ashes were strewn.

A quote from Shakespeare was etched on his ruins,
a wife and three daughters, mourning and hurt,
he'd trained as an astronaut for the moon -
there on the surface, his ashes were strewn.

Kissing grandma

Slowly, the sea, of black suits
and mourning dresses, parted,
allowing the small boy through,
the prone woman there on view,
a daughter holding his hand;
his mother. He kneels down,
on carpeted stair, staring
at old fingers, rosary.
The abyss of coffin falls
away, the child staggering
down dark vertigo,
clinging to the larger hand.
*It's alright, honey, say 'bye
to Nana* – his mother's voice,
thin, choked, in her suffering,
the elder woman, once large,
now compressed into a black-
boxed rectangle of Lily,
the impossibly large breasts,
gone girlish, pressed and flattened,
this cold relic, not quite her.
What is missing? Her laughter,
as she leads small me downstairs,
to basement kitchen, fragrant
with frying perch, oil, sauces,
a white stove, and coal furnace,
the canning room, where bottles

of yellow peppers, peaches,
tomatoes, cellar light-lit,
under low ceiling, a round
eating table, the plastic
protecting the embroidered
and full-bodied linen cloth,
sewn during her hard war years -
four sons left home, to fight, three
returned, *my tears fell into
every stitch*, she told me.
No crying now, my eyes wide
wondering watching fixed to
horror silence mystery.
It is her but it is not.
The grandma part has drained out.
Kiss her now, and say goodbye -
my mother's voice so soft,
so high, above my bowed head,
I lean across polished wood,
gripping the cold brass handle,
my smaller lips brushing hers,
briefly tasting foundation,
as I'm gently pulled away.

Chả ốc

My partner had a moment -
tucking into the thick Hanoi omelet -

enquiring as to its composition.
Our host, Lien, indicated the English translation

on the menu—as I
read aloud—Snail Pie.

Chewing stopped mid-bite.
She discreetly extracted the rubbery mite,

with pinched fingertips,
delicately placing it on plate lip.

I remembered fascination as a child,
my grandmother cooking wild

garden variety in our basement kitchen,
their attempted escape bid bewitching,

as they crawled out, hot
from her slippery steel cooking pot,

down the side, before grandma's pinching,
in a similar way, their desperate inching,

and, with casual toss,
threw them back into the sauce.

The ballad of true and false singing

When a tiny quail huddled beneath the wall
proclaims quiet poetry in her call,
I cannot hear louder songs at all,
for singing big is not always how
          the singing's measured,
but often by the soul
                that's still and true,
Maestro-singers reveal treasured
declamations of God's perfect view.
Few possess it young
but all become Masters yet
in verse, ballad or canzonet.

Ah! a world of Maestros of every grace -
the poor student can barely find a place.

anonymous – from the Italian – translated by Joe Dolce

Aloysius' lament
in memoriam Les Murray, 1938 – 2019

Master is gone, the Apprentice forlorn,
his unfinished works, shadowed, in repose -
the mentor has died; a mentor is born.

The cauldron is cold that fired the morn,
his watchful eye, so sharp yet so kind, closed,
Master is gone, the Apprentice forlorn.

Grief smothers the day, the heart's page is torn,
so small in death, his white hair, a white rose,
the mentor has died; a mentor is born.

He left you complete and found you half-formed.
Works you presented, so many he chose,
Master is gone, the Apprentice forlorn.

There is no tomorrow, the soul is sore,
the beloved's fled, you cannot follow,
the mentor has died; a mentor is born.

Pick up your tools, Aloysius, and soar,
there's much you must give, before you can go.
Master is gone, the Apprentice forlorn -
the mentor has died; a mentor is born.

Empty strollers

Standing on Przemyśl platform
seven quiet empty strollers,
remote from the Russian war-storm,
left for Ukrainian mothers,

fleeing the fight with small children,
at the border crossing between
Ukraine and Poland, seven prams
filled with blankets and warm clothing,

by Polish parents' donation,
refusing to bear mind-blindness,
left at Przemyśl Station,
spurring the world to choose kindness.

*

One hundred nine empty strollers,
in Lviv, placed in Rynok mall,
a message to Russian mothers -
remember your children when small,

in neat rows, one for each child killed
empty prams never to be filled.

*

One hundred wet empty pushers,
in San Francisco's Chrissy Field,
protesting the babies butchered,
in the Russian invasion, killed.

In sympathy, left on the field
in that rainy weekend downpour,
remembering, and unconcealed,
the shameful artifacts of war.

The ballad of William Crowe

My own true love was decent,
as good as good men go,
bad fortune turned him bittersweet,
my husband, William Crowe.

Mother often begged me,
'Oh Sal, why won't you go?'
I couldn't quit that battering man,
my husband, William Crowe.

He hit me with his hand and fist,
when he was in whisky,
then gave me a white faux fur coat,
and apologized to me.

I turned my face so many times,
I pleaded with him so,
he never changed his bruising ways,
my husband, William Crowe.

I snuck his Johnnie Walker,
(he was too drunk to know),
half-filled it up with RatSak while
he watched his late night show.

The bedroom was so quiet,
he slept and never woke,
I poisoned-dead that battering man,
my husband, William Crowe.

My mother's at her window,
her face no more I'll see,
that jury's word was cold as hell -
the needle waits for me.

Oh darling mother, find me, pray,
in Heaven's afterglow,
for I have killed a battering man,
whose name is William Crowe.

In repose

In the water she lay in repose,
the hot bath always a quiet time,
her arm was stiff, the water was cold.

Many nights we often slept alone,
she in her small bed and I in mine,
in the water she lay in repose.

Up for toilet, my regular stroll,
three am bathroom ritual time,
her arm was stiff, the water was cold.

The flame had turned the tea-kettle gold,
glowing in the dark and boiled dry,
in the water she lay in repose.

She seemed fast asleep, her eyes were closed.
Wake up darling, I felt for some sign,
her arm was stiff, the water was cold.

Wake up darling! my voice uncontrolled,
her mouth just below the water line.
In the water she lay in repose,
her arm was stiff, the water was cold.

Don Diego's Accordion

Don Diego's accordion

I quit childhood accordion lessons
due to a time conflict with Zorro
my favourite b&w tv show of the 50s
three slashes of sword
whishhht! whishhht! whishhht!
like the sign of the cross
cut a Z into many young hearts
I hung up the rapier and bullwhip
shortly after George W Bush was run
out of town on the back of El Toro
but occasionally don the black cape and mask
to help local townspeople
with corrupt politicians and greedy landowners
and for infrequent shopping mall appearances
Zorro Spanish for fox pronounced soro
credited with inspiration
by their respective creators
for The Lone Ranger and Batman
whereas the accordion inspired
the blind and the file
I think I made the right choice.

Gluten-free toast

May your Third Eye   remain open
giving you   20-20-20 vision.
May your Vishnu   always be New,
your Tantric   always be Tricky,
your Gita   always be Sweeta,
your 2nd hand Karma's   front end,
(and your Chakras)   have perfect alignment

and may you stay   forever Jung.

Clearly not Fourth Street

With your fish hook mouth in the bottom-feeder times,
and your eyes like marbles and your skin like rind,
and your silver scales and your sermon that whines,
Oh, who among the fishermen could fry you?

With your pockets full of correct tokens at last,
but the streetcar departing that you missed when it passed,
and your lizard-like run for it, and your pencil moustache,
who among your black girlfriends wouldn't untie you?

With your trail mix nuts and your pumpkin seeds,
and the tarot cards you never learned to read,
and your op shop hats and gold jumper leads,
you need a 12-volt battery to jump-start you.

With your silo eyes where the wheat is loaded,
and your tractor head with the gears eroded,
and your ga-ga writing with the words encoded,
you say you never read poetry 'cause it's too hard to.

The Queen of Typhus in her hospital cot,
is third in line for her penicillin shot,
and the big toe on your left foot is starting to rot,
while you wonder which nurse will take you out,

and the mounting flames in your pyjama attire,
from your cigarette ash that started a fire,
but you were too stoned on coke to enquire,
the name of the fireman who put you out.

Oh, the poets and geriatrics all met on the cliff,
to determine if you were dead or limp or just stiff,
and why did you steal that Muddy Waters riff,
that you'd think we're so deaf, it's bewildering.

Well, I wish you'd never left Maggie's Farm,
but I'll walk you back there, if you just take my arm,
but first autograph this rabbit-foot charm,
and a photo to give to my children.

Now you hold that honorary PhD,
you try to be humble, but you know you're still mean,
you crank out those albums just like a machine,
as long as your agent gets bookins'.

With your baby-faced lips and your curly hair, too,
and your tight peg-legged jeans and your spit-polished boot,
you KNOW what Allen Ginsberg really wanted to do,
every time you bent over, he was lookin'.

Constellation

Victoria's Secret Dylan.
Las Vegas Elvis.
Toupéed Sinatra.
Nose-lifted Jackson.
Door-hung Hutchinson.

Five Emperors repose indolently,
in Elysium, or Hell, or Nowhere,
attended, foot and hand,
by tattooed cherubim roadies.
Four have nodded off,
the fifth releases Sacred Wind.
The gallery genuflects.

Meanwhile, Somewhere,
five children gaze out windows
of midnight schoolrooms,
lesson-bored, staring in awe
at the star dome above,
imagining how one day
they might jigsaw,
their glittering pieces,
into Cassiopeia, Chamaeleon, Triangulum.

Starvation box blues

When I got myself this Starvation Box
my daddy told me son you're bound to lose
you ain't never gonna make no money playing that guitar
only give you the Starvation Box blues.

Now I've stood in that Welfare line
I've passed the hat and I've played for food
I hope my luck changes soon
I'm sick of these Starvation Box blues.

Sometimes I want to smash this Starvation Box
build a fire just to warm my feet
or bust it into little pieces
and use the toothpicks to pick my teeth.

My music has got me through some hard times
music has made me jump and shout
this Starvation Box has been my best friend for so long
Lord I just can't turn it out.

Sometimes I wish I had me a regular job
and was making steady money just like you
instead of living with so much damn uncertainty
and all these Starvation Box blues.

Gingerbread house

Two out of the past three
nights have been therapy nights:
shortcomings, character flaws,
thorough analysis of every member
of both our families,
self-criticism, allegation, hearsay,
emotional manipulation and interpretations,
all braided together deftly with praise,
empowerment, forgiveness,
strategic turning of thoughts elsewhere,
and renewal of vows.
The soundtrack to this marvellous film:
torrential rain drumming on corrugated iron,
a wood-smoke fireplace *aria*
and sudden *crescendo* of darkness to sleep.
Al fine.

The next morning, the thorough workout
behind us, love glimmers brilliantly
of renewal, first days, origins –

before poisoned fruit,
bread-crumbed forest walks.

Fracture

A small thing.
Insignificant, really.
Out of play, or spite, the crossing
of a line no one saw, a slight -
imagined or real - a single hairline
crack. At first, a bruise, a smart,
built-up pressure beneath
pushing edges apart.
Some space, some denial, some bandaging.
Family resumes as before.
The mark fades.

Out of nowhere,
another unexpected collision,
this time, more severe. Cracks reappear,
the fissure opens, edges widening,
too far to bridge
with practiced panacea.
Words fail.
What was caged is now freed,
a fatal breech.
Years of silence

I said left, at the fork, Robert - *Left!*

Two roads diverged in a wood, and I –
I took the one more travelled by,
and that has made no difference whatsoever.

Topophilia with Leunig at Officeworks

A sense of place results gradually and unconsciously from inhabiting a landscape over time becoming familiar with its physical properties, accruing history within its confines.
Kent Rydon

He was taller
than the little cartoon figure
I imagined

conversation started randomly
in the checkout queue
stringwound out into the parking lot

leaning against respective beat-up cars
whirling through eclectic matters
with the speed of pensioners playing one-armed bandits

the obscurity of modern Australian poetry
the art of setting-words-to-music
until the three cherries abruptly stopped

on Rydon's idea of a sense of place in one's work
the Wales of Dylan Thomas Les Murray's Bunyah
Faulkner in Yoknapatawpha County

Shinto kami
even dis-placed aboriginal artists
have it in every brush stroke

could transplanted souls
have this in their new adopted country
without crutching in childhood memories

we agreed (I think) the true visionary
would see the rose as Adam saw it
even in car-clogged concrete surrounding us

a perceptive person would note the genius loci
of our very conversation instil that spirit of place
in music poem or drawing

as we said our good-byes and shook hands
I noticed a fleck of white
paint on Leunig's nose

I restrained the dresser in me
from reaching up
and brushing it off.

Note: Michael Leunig is an Australian poet, cartoonist and cultural commentator. His best known works include The Adventures of Vasco Pyjama and the Curly Flats series. He was declared an Australian Living Treasure by the National Trust of Australia in 1999.

Dumb phones

I miss them.
You left them home.
You didn't stare into them at lunch.
You put your finger
in the ring and rotated it.
It rang like a phone,
not like an ice cream truck.
It doubled as a weapon -
when you hit someone,
it didn't bounce off.
You knocked them out.

They were dumb,
but they weren't stupid.

Catoptromancy
For now we see through a glass darkly... 1 Corinthians 13:12

Divination with mirrors,
priests called *specularii*,
practiced by Emperon Didius Julianus,
the Achaeans, besiegers of Troy.
The first were pools of dark, still water.
John Dee, 16th century mathematician,
occult astrologer, used polished obsidian.
Dr Raymond Moody, originator of the term
near-death experience,
sat in a chamber —the *psychomanteum* -
surfaces angled to reflect only darkness.

Mirror mirror on the wall.
Bad luck to break one.
Traditionally covered, after death.
Ancestor of the selfie.

Wolf

Two-note glissando,
rising and falling pitch,
heard by every woman,
passing a building site.
Whoot whoo,
wheet whoo.
Debate as to origins -
the Navy, turn to,
sounded with boatswain's pipe,
or Albanian sheep-dog call,
shepherds warning of predators.
Eve-teasing, in Asia -
with its own emoji.
Soon to be extinct,
France considering a 90 Euro fine,
#MeToo might be the final nail.

First popularized by animator
Tex Avery's 1943 Red Hot Riding Hood:
the wolf hoots Red,
tongue lolling, eyes popping out of head.
Avery's work favoured
by US military during WWII:
increased libido, from sexy cartoons,
created frustration, aggression,
better soldiers.

Sheila Harrod, 74, world champion whistler,
would like to hear a few more:
you don't have it much now –
people fear harassment.
It's a shame - I always thought it cheeky.
If someone did it to me,
I'd do it back twice as loud -
that'd always get a laugh.

Rubik's paradelle

Picasso made people jig saw puzzles.
Picasso made people jig saw puzzles.
Doctor Frankenstein stitched body parts together.
Doctor Frankenstein stitched body parts together.
Doctor Picasso stitched jig people parts.
Frankenstein saw body puzzles made together.

Butchers chop animal apart in pieces.
Butchers chop animal apart in pieces.
Rubik's Cube has six painted faces.
Rubik's Cube has six painted faces.
Painted butchers Cube has animal faces
in six Rubik's chop apart pieces.

Three hidden personalities of Eve.
Three hidden personalities of Eve.
Tricky dating some psycho bitch.
Tricky dating some psycho bitch.
Dating bitch Psycho Eve,
some three personalities of hidden tricky.

Saw doctor has six Frankenstein faces.
Tricky Picasso hidden psycho personalities.
Butcher bitch made dating people puzzles,
three body pieces chop apart,
Rubik's animal jig some of Eve,
stitched together in painted Cube parts.

Note: The Paradelle is a demanding fixed-form poem, invented by Billy Collins. It consists of four six-line stanzas in which the first and second lines, as well as the third and four lines, of the first three stanzas, must be identical. The fifth and sixth lines, of each stanza, must use all the words, from the first and third lines of the stanza, and only those words. Similarly, the final stanza must use every word, from lines 1,3,7,9,13 and 15, of the preceding stanzas and only those words.

Muse-wrestling

Starting as a mere arm wrestle,
differences quickly escalate,
to chokeholds around a cliché,
       flipping it, like a back-on-its-turtle.

Quickly, squared off on hands and knees,
Prose braces itself; Poetry
hunches over the diagrammed
       spine; referee slaps the mat, grunt and tug

explodes in collar-and-elbow,
face-and-heel, and a double turn,
Prose is lifted, then a head drop,
       into a pin, a kick-out frees meter.

Poetry, dazed from its blown spot,
has a small cut above a rhyme.
The fighters circle each other,
       tired, hunting weakness, or no contest.

Verse, bloodied, loses its balance,
tripping on adverbs, a near-fall -
Prose throws an illegal head-lock!
       THREE COUNT! - the referee lifts Poetry's hand.

# The Cavafy Villanelles

Prost

May you live to be a hundred years with one extra year to repent. -Irish toast

Let us lower our glasses.
To the grumbletonians and ultracrepidarians;
mugwmps engaged in jargoyled trumpery,
zwoddered cockalorums and snollygosters,
purveyors of twaddle and fudgel,
callipygian lanspesados,
(exuding shivviness),
in elflock and groke.

Let us lower our glasses.
To adversaries.
May they overcome chronic dysania,
to expire in crapulous throes
of hubris and hum durgeon.

I never found those lips again

I never found those lips again
my final preference for her kiss
I never thought that I could bend

when she had gone it felt the end
sorrow broke open an abyss
I never found those lips again

kind words from a few mutual friends
who didn't vanish into mist
I never thought that I could bend

some lovers with a soft pretend
their touch somehow always amiss
I never found those lips again

the helpful advice that offends
(there still too much I won't dismiss)
I never thought that I could bend

an almost heal but never mend
the unannounced recall of bliss
I never found those lips again
I never thought that I could bend.

Roll-your-own Lamb

Bereft of kindling newsprint,
being a particularly cold bush night,
reluctantly, I reached for the dry leaves
of the Oxford Book of Light Verse.

Ripping out Publication Details,
Index of Lines, I began
lighting Kipling, Butler and Yeats,
pausing at DH Lawrence,
tearing Pope, Swift, Anon.

When cigarette papers ran out,
a real conundrum:
with whom would I share breath?

I chose Charles Lamb's, A Farewell to Tobacco,
a fine poem, no doubt a fine smoke.
If cancer were to fog an x-ray,
no worthier bloke.

Scissoring a rectangle, from ...*more from a mistress than a weed*...
down to ...*while thou suck'st the lab'ring breath*...
I tobacco'd up, rolling
and thread-tying a beedi.

Inhaling, I watched the orange edge
erasing phrases,
sooty retainer to the vine, vanishing,
more and greater oaths to break, becoming ash.
The burning poem pinched my fingers;
I stubbed it out.

Nicotine-dazed, eyes closed,
I raised supplication to the poet.

I might smoke Edward Lear next.

Bach blind

Short-sighted since childhood
over-zealous self-taught
dusk to dawn copying scores
by lamplight by poor light
hand cramped tireless and prolific
grown old his vision worsening
in pain and nowhere else to turn
and he wanted to go on serving God

peripatetic English doctor Chevalier Taylor
specialist and oculist renown ophthalmiater
notorious for innovative cataract needles
the operation called couching
not complicated nor expensive no guarantee

lie on your back
strapped to leather bench head in restraint
two assistants held shoulders knees
a third insured eyelids remained open
quickly deftly thick sharply pointed needle
jabbed into eye probing slightly
reaching lens pushing downward quickly
into vitreous jelly
with only whisky to numb pain
a scream of utter agony every bit of strength
of three men required to restrain thrashing

afterwards wound bathed
in Peruvian balsam warm water
cataplasm of cassia pulp
eye fomented with spirituous camphire
bandage replaced by patch
eat lightly with gentle evacuations

Bach recovered his eyesight fully
a few days later a second operation
the horror of the procedure repeated this time with
no good result attributed *to advanced condition*
bottom was found to be defective
a paralytic disorder - had he come earlier and so forth

the eyesight deteriorated quickly after that
he woke up one morning in darkness
after that spent hours days
just sitting in a darkened room
composing in his head
remembering light

Knife penny

Stir with a knife and stir up strife. anon

Never close a knife if someone else has opened it.
Two knives crossed on an Irish table cause a quarrel.
Two knives crossed on an Italian table insult the Cross.
A knife crossed with a spoon indicates bad food - curse on the cook.
A knife in a cradle's headboard guards the baby.
Black-handled knives under Grecian pillows keep away nightmares.
Bad luck to say the word *knife* while at sea.
Bad luck to buy a knife and not first cut wood or paper.
Bad fortune to sharpen a blade in Mississippi after sundown.
Bad omen to scour a butcher's knife.
Good fortune to find a knife, no matter how useless and old - keep it.
A Russian knife lying sharp side up augurs the birth of a murderer.
A knife left lying on its back cuts an angel's foot.
Playing with a Romanian knife causes an angel to flee.
Licking food off a Ukrainian knife makes you cruel and angry like a dog.
Sleeping above a Chinese knife scares away evil spirits.
Presenting a knife to a Japanese colleague suggests suicide.
Navajo knives are used only to cut, never to stab food, or as forks.
Dull knives, in Jamaican kitchens, indicate husband's worthlessness in bed.
Touching oneself with a knife, in Madagascar, causes leprosy.
A knife in a jar of water wards off evil spirits afraid of reflections.
A knife given as a gift severs friendship - unless a coin is taped to the blade.
A combat knife placed back in its sheath before drawing blood will fail you in battle.
A Chinese knife that has slain a person is precious.
You never truly own a knife until it has bitten you.

Barbarians

This morning, after tea
and chapatis, we stripped
the bed, our pyjamas,
linens, anything made of cloth,
and boiled the lot.

While asleep, a battalion
of dust mites chewed
a crimson swath across
our thighs and backs.

Citronella over the bed frame,
Aerogard on the mattress,
sheets and spreads fly
wild from clothes lines.

As bedtime arrives,
everything reassembled,
in colourful order,
somewhat sleepless,
we await the next wave
of ambitious barbarians.

Homage to Shead
after Homage to Rembrandt, *by Garry Shead*

Come now, Erato, and I'll tell you, not
of Matthew's angel, Jacob's wrestling,
the Shepherds' vision, or old Abraham's
entertainments, departures from Tobit
and Tobias; nor will you see phantoms
of the Master's darkness, the three of four
children dead (with their mother), seductions
of nurse and maid, the pauper's burial;
not chiaroscuro's light and umbra,
but Boyd's Tinkerbell muse, held by a leg,
the painter's eyes closed, about to be slapped,
Saskia/Judith watching at the door.

Yubitsume
Yubi o tobasu (He made his finger fly)

Finger shortening.
Ritual introduced in 17th century,
by *bakuto* gamblers,
feudal forerunners of *yakuza*
(ya-ku-sa, the worst possible hand
in the card game, *Oicho-Kabu*.)
Atonement for offenses to another,
to show sincere apology, by means
of amputation of portions
of one's own little finger.
In Kendo, finger-amputees,
unable to grip swords properly,
became more reliant on protection
of *oyabun* (foster parent).

The left hand,
determined by Japanese culture,
forbidding left-handedness, is laid,
onto a small clean cloth, face-down.
The *kobun* (foster child), with a sharp *tantō*,
cuts above top knuckle.
The severed tip (*iki yubi* –
living finger), wrapped in cloth,
is graciously submitted to the *oyabun*.

Further offenses require further joints.

Vitis vinifera

The sway of alcohol over mankind is unquestionably due to its power to stimulate the mystical faculties of human nature usually crushed to earth by the cold facts and dry criticism of the sober hours.
        -*William James*, The Varieties of Religious Experience, 1902.

Did a drunken Noah receive instructions
or was the gopherwood felled in sober hours?
Vinum fuelled the songs of Homer,
the poetry of Alcman,
brimmed Tutankhamun's amphora.
Maurya practiced tantra on Madhu.
Certain Sunni Hanafi ferment
dates for medicinal purposes.
The Kiddush sanctifies four cups,
a Rabbinical obligation on Pesach.

King James anointed wine a mocker,
beer the brawler's inebriation,
a symbol of God's wrath,
yet Jesus' first miracle turned it,
glasses lifted at the Supper.

Fingering clay figurines of Bacchus,
Romans planted the vineyards of Bordeaux.

Korean triptych

i. Sōshi-kaimei

occupiers gone
Confucius removes
jade mask

ii. Jeo

in Shi Jing poems
kimchi reduces wrinkles:
silkskin grandmother

iii. Carpodacus Roseus

feathers of dawn cross
the 38th parallel
lost Pallas' Rosefinch

* Koreans forced to take Japanese surnames were referred to as sōshi-kaimei.
* Jeo: early name for kimchi.
* Shi Jing: Book of Songs, first Chinese poetry book 1000 BC.
* Pallas' Rosefinch (carpodacus roseus) is native to both North and South Korea.

Narcissus shaving in the river

While it's true, he was cursed
to fall for that bearded boy
in the water-mirror,

this newly clean-shaven youth
mysteriously free from the witchy-will,
of that bitch Nemesis,
now returns to unfettered indulgence.

The Cavafy Villanelles

1. Fifty-nine retired

Fifty-nine retired   he hated clerking,
on his final day   friends heard him exclaim -
At last! I am freed   from the despised thing.

Three decades behind   a desk accounting,
the mournful line   of monotonous days,
fifty-nine retired,   he hated clerking.

Months pressed into years   such an endless string,
feeling like a poet   only in name -
At last! I am freed   from the despised thing.

He hoped to write more   without stunted wings,
a hundred voices inside   to declaim,
fifty-nine retired   he hated clerking.

The Ministry   of Irrigation's din,
passing in distant echoes   out of frame -
At last! I am freed   from the despised thing.

More time for books   and free time for writing,
more late night strolls   to neighbourhood cafés,
fifty-nine retired   he hated clerking -
At last! I am freed   from the despised thing.

2. Hericleia

His sister Helen died   at one year old,
Heracleia wanted   a daughter -
for years his mother   dressed him in girl's clothes.

Her older sons were grown   and uncontrolled,
this child was her joy   until she lost her -
his sister Helen died   at one year old.

In buttoned dresses   crinoline and bows,
in fantasy   she recreated her,
for years his mother   dressed him in girl's clothes.

His mother heard her voice   from the shadows,
addled damaged   there her demons fought her,
his sister Helen died   at one year old.

Reclusive Heracleia   grew old,
he worked until she died   to support her,
for years his mother   dressed him in girl's clothes.

The tone of poems   that he would soon compose
was tempered in the years   she haunted her,
his sister Helen died   at one year old,
for years his mother   dressed him in girl's clothes.

3. At the noisy café

He sits alone   at the noisy café,
old age a wound   from a terrible knife -
he was younger it seems   just yesterday.

The hair dye has hidden   most of the grey,
how suddenly it came   this change-of-life,
he sits alone   at the noisy café.

A table-for-one   a vase and bouquet,
without children   a companion or wife -
he was younger it seems   just yesterday.

He gives friends photos   of his younger days,
to help them recall him   in kinder light,
he sits alone   at the noisy café.

He's thrown so many   early poems away,
clearly too consumed   with lust then to write -
he was younger it seems   just yesterday.

Now almost transparent,   thoughts far away,
a breeze of Eros   sweeps past in the night,
he sits alone   at the noisy café -
he was younger it seems   just yesterday.

4. Days of 1926

The Order of the Phoenix   carried weight,
presented by   General Pangolos,
to return it   would insult the Greek State.

Dictator Prime Minister   Head of State,
in that year he vanquished   all who opposed -
the Order of the Phoenix   carried weight.

A bloodless coup   let Pangolos dictate,
when King Constantine the First   was deposed,
to refuse it   would insult the Greek State.

Bestowed on Greek artists   to celebrate
high excellence   in poetry and prose,
the Order of the Phoenix   carried weight.

May 13th 1926   the date
the first medal laureates   were disclosed -
to refuse it   would insult the Greek State.

At age sixty-three   to commemorate
works the poet had been proud   to compose,
The Order of the Phoenix   carried weight,
to return it   would insult the Greek State.

5. Bath

His body   responding in ecstasy,
recalls caresses   he once knew in youth,
he abandons himself   to reverie.

In the bath, the low-light   his senses free,
indulgent again   (there is no excuse!)
his old body   responds in ecstasy.

Calming sore muscles   his tired body
allowing candle-lit water   to soothe,
he abandons himself   to reverie.

Too much Eros   (he wouldn't disagree),
too many cigarettes   too much vermouth,
his old body   responds in ecstasy.

So long ago   now a dim memory,
there was one singular lad   that amused,
he abandons himself   to reverie.

With salts and oils   steaming the glass at ease,
there in the dark   in the low-light diffused,
his body   responding in ecstasy,
he abandons himself   to reverie.

6. Literati

The London literati   were impressed,
when E.M. Forster   commended his poems,
Leonard Woolf wanted him   for Hogarth Press!

He'd rented a flat   on Rue Lepsisus,
above a brothel   where he lived alone.
The London literati   were impressed.

T.E. Lawrence   was an enthusiast,
but thought the poet   should translate his own.
Leonard Woolf wanted him   for Hogarth Press.

In Toynbee's The Nation   he was published.
Robert Graves visited him   at his home.
The London literati   were impressed.

Over Lawrence Durrell   his spell was cast,
Siegfried Sassoon wrote -   "anxious for more poems" -
Leonard Woolf wanted him   for Hogarth Press.

Reviews in the New Statesman   and the rest,
in The Times   Middleton Murry intoned.
The London literati   were impressed -
Leonard Woolf wanted him   for Hogarth Press!

7. Ithaca

'Penelope's fidelity   the throne,
a son - those yearnings   strengthened his resolve,
to return to Ithaca   and his home.

Ten years of war   ten years in the unknown,
past Circe the Cyclops.   His only salve? -
Penelope's fidelity   the throne.

Poseidon cursed   Odysseus to roam,
to fight Troy his own   Labours to be solved,
before return to Ithaca   his home.'

Ithaca. The poet's   most well-known poem.
Why diminish the prize   how it resolved -
Penelope's fidelity   his throne?

Of course, our Odysseus   would have known
the long 'beautiful voyage'   would dissolve
on return to Ithaca   to his home.

A naïve poem   revision might atone.
Odysseus' struggles   were absolved -
Penelope's fidelity   the throne,
on return to Ithaca   and his home.

8. Almost mythical

To make the visible   invisible
is the pleasure of the young   but old age
can turn the invisible   visible.

Young beauties   ideal and unmissable
seek out each other   in forbidden ways
to make the visible   invisible.

The old poet   his flesh miserable
robs his memory   recalling past days
to turn the invisible   visible.

Ephemeral youth   almost mythical
with lips and skin entwined   burns such a blaze
to make the visible   invisible.

The old ones wounded   inconsolable
find solace in work   reverie and praise
to turn the invisible   visible.

Poetry, Eros   make life liveable
Youth burns tomorrow   the Old yesterdays -
to make the visible   invisible
and turn the invisible   visible.

9. Nyktoporia 1932

His lifelong addiction   to cigarettes
brought him to   glorious Athens again,
he suffered from   cancer of the larynx.

He had dismissed it   of no consequence,
the hoarseness of the chronic   cough and pain -
his lifelong addiction   to cigarettes.

The loss of his voice   was his main regret,
the tracheotomy   (nothing remained),
he suffered from   cancer of the larynx.

No longer able to smoke   or forget
those sublime exhales   (the nicotine stains!)
his lifelong addiction   to cigarettes.

Strong Turkish tobacco   helped him relax
but the surgery   forced him to abstain,
he suffered from   cancer of the larynx.

His voice gone, with reverie   he reflects
on nocturnal walks   in warm Athens rain,
his lifelong addiction   to cigarettes,
he suffered from   cancer of the larynx.

10. Last embrace of Alexandria

It's as though   he had never been away,
this last embrace   of Alexandria.
The funeral of the poet   was today.

His birth city   on this marvellous day,
the blooms in April   of wisteria,
it's as though   he had never been away.

Six years education   sent him away,
youth in the England   of Victoria.
The funeral of the poet   was today.

Fine incense and candles   kneeling to pray,
the angels holding   hexapteriga,
it's as though   he had never been away.

Icons honouring   the Byzantine way,
a liturgical choir   the Glorias,
the funeral of the poet   was today.

Soft Hellenic amber   ending the day,
across the hills   of Alexandria,
it's as though   he had never been away.
The funeral of the poet   was today.

And ever shall be

The fireworks cosmos is spinning,
will Mars be sanctuary -
our souls to mend?

> *As it was in the beginning,*
> *is now and ever shall be,*
> *world without end.*

The virus appears winning -
(does life depend on the bee?)
can we defend?

> *As it was in the beginning,*
> *is now and ever shall be,*
> *world without end.*

Is AI praying or sinning,
who, or what, will hear our plea -
our next Godsend?

> *As it was in the beginning,*
> *is now and ever shall be,*
> *world without end.*

If breathable air is thinning,
(did we evolve from the sea?)
can humans bend?

> *As it was in the beginning,*
> *is now and ever shall be,*
> *world without end.*

Some claim the fabric's unpinning -
the dinosaur- or the flea.
Then how? Or when?

> *As it was in the beginning,*
> *is now and ever shall be,*
> *world without end.*

author's statement

Aloysius's lament was written for Les Murray AO on the day he passed away.

My family was Catholic and faithful church goers. Every Sunday, like clockwork. I went to a public school but on Saturday mornings, I was required to attend religious training at our local St Mary's Church. Luckily, the church also had a large basketball auditorium that was used for afternoon roller-skating, which I also attended faithfully, so I consider myself a lapsed Catholic but a practicing roller-skater.

I had my First Communion, at eight years old, and when it came time for my Confirmation, shortly afterwards, I was told I could pick my own Confirmation name. I was unaccustomed to this kind of religious freedom and 'free will'. The Catholic clergy in our small Ohio town was pretty strict. We weren't allowed to walk directly in front of the local Protestant churches – we had to cross the street. One new kid in class one day added the traditional Protestant closing to the Lord's Prayer: 'for thine is the kingdom, the power, and the glory, for ever and ever,' and the nun walked over and slapped him.

I had an eraser thrown at me by an angry Sister once when I laughed out loud on hearing that Adam and Eve probably ate insects in the Garden of Eden!

I looked around through the various books on Saints lives and decided on Aloysius for my Confirmation name; my full Catholic name becoming Joseph Michael Aloysius Dolce.

St Aloysius de Gonzaga was born an Italian aristocrat. His parents were members of the Royal Courts of Italy and Spain. I think I remember choosing his name because I was moved that he gave up a large inheritance to become a Jesuit, and that he was the patron saint of young students. His motto was *born for greater things*. It's a pleasant coincidence that my favourite verse from the Bible, in later years, became Jesus' words, in John 14:12, 'Truly, truly, I say to you, whoever believes in me will also do the works that I do; and *greater works* than these will he do.'

I learned years later that *Aloysius* came from the Germanic word meaning 'famous warrior' and that St Aloysius was also the patron saint of plague victims. When the plague broke out in Rome, in 1591, he worked in a Jesuit hospital for victims, where he died, of the illness, at 23 years old. He was canonized in 1726, by Pope Benedict XIII.

Seventeen of the poems included here are villanelles. I began my relationship with creative language as a songwriter and I developed my skills as a poet primarily in the service of a better song-lyric. The villanelle, or villanesque, is one of the most effective structures for a songwriter to write strong poetic lyrics. It originated in France in the 1600s, as a ballad, but over the centuries evolved into simple poetic scaffolding, due to its fixed form, for stand-alone poetry, as in Dylan Thomas's classic, *Do Not Go Gentle Into That Good Night*.

I have returned it to its origins. The repetitive lines lend themselves to hypnotic, almost obsessive themes and the result is uncannily always musical in nature. I have already created songs from two of the poems, *The murder of Alberta King* and *I never found those lips again*, as well as many others not included here.

All the poems, lyrics and the libretto, in this volume, have appeared in poetry journals. The one exception is the *Cavafy villanelles*. Only three, of the ten, have been previously published, so far, but I feel the group works best as a whole, rather than fragmented.

The late Les Murray, in his role as an editor, once asked me to send him more of my humorous poems (as I guess he wasn't getting enough laughs) so I trust I have included, scattered here and there, enough of his favourite Shakespearean elements of misconception, reason versus emotion, fate and the fantastical, idyllic setting, insult, separation and reconciliation - and happy endings.

Joe Dolce, North Carlton 2023.

special acknowledgments

To *Dan Guenther*, for his sustained poetic encouragement, generous friendship, and inspiring leadership for well over a decade; to *Elizabeth Smither*, for a perfect book title and being a good pen pal; to *Dave Mason*, for his musical appreciation and our mutual appreciation of moussaka and Cavafy - and the romantic courage to fall in love with another poet; to *Geoff Page*, for his unique narrative poetic voice and for taking me into **Best Australian Poems**, twice; to *Andrew Lansdown*, for thoughtful prayers and deep thoughts on samurai and Bob Dylan; to *Suzanne Edgar*, for introducing me to both the villanelle *and* Les Murray - two utter life changers; to *Barry Spurr*, for selecting, and publishing, thirty-five of the poems in this volume, for successfully taking over the impossible position of poetry editor of **Quadrant** and for his ongoing belief in my work; to *Penelope Cottier* and *Akua Lezli Hope* for 'groking' my love for science fiction things - in *all* things; to *Melinda Smith*, *John Foulcher*, and again to Geoff and Penelope, for graciously welcoming me to Canberra poetry; to *George Thomas*, for thirteen years of looking over my shoulder as a creative editor; to *Kris Hemensley*, for the poet's introduction; to *Donna Ward*, for unearthing my Leunig poem, out of a blind submission, when no one else could, (even with eyes open), and for bringing the late Les Murray over for dinner, for some of my home-cooked pig tails and red-eye gravy (his request!) and, finally, to our endlessly-missed *Blaise van Hecke*, and *Kev Howlett*, *Les Zig* and **Busybird Publishing** for this little book, which was a too-long time coming.

publication history

All poems first published in **Quadrant** magazine, except:

Kero aphrodesia, *Dumb phones* and *Gall revisited*. Canberra Times.
Painting and *Homage to Shead*, Verity La.
Stepdaughter, Journey.
Our loss, Grieve.
Don Diego's accordion and *Horsewitch*, Contrappasso.
Shoemaker's moon, Ginninderra Press, *Milestones* anthology.
The sound of one shear clicking and *Chả ốc*, Green Door.
Roll-your-own Lamb, North of Oxford (US).
Car with the lot, University of Canberra Vice-Chancellor's Poetry Prize, *Silence* anthology.
Broad Arrow Café, University of Canberra Vice-Chancellor's Poetry Prize, *Signs* anthology.
And let the wonder in, University of Canberra Vice-Chancellor's Health Poetry Prize, First Place, Meniscus: *Volume 5, Issue 2*.
Vase, Newcastle Poetry Prize, *Measures of Truth* anthology.
Starvation box blues, Overland.
Enitharmon's bower, ACU Poetry Prize, *Generosity* anthology.
The tyger, Australian Poetry Journal.
Le grand masked ball of phantasmagoric Melbourne, City of Melbourne Poet Laureates anthology.
Carmenta'lia, Carmenta.
Korean triptych, Cordite.
Aliens, Eye to the Telescope 2
Unfathomable, Eye to the Telescope 42
Bach blind, Antipodes (US).
A toast to free verse, The Crow.
And ever shall be, Live Encounters.
Topophilia with Leunig at Officeworks, Sotto.
Go for it, Joe! © Kris Hemensley, Your Scratch Entourage, Cordite Books, 2016.

about the author

Joe Dolce is a composer and poet and an Australian-American dual national.

He was a 2021 City of Melbourne Poet Laureate, Highly Commended in the 2020 ACU Poetry Prize, short-listed in 2020 & 2014 Newcastle Poetry Prizes, short-listed in the 2019, 2018, 2017 & 2014 University of Canberra Vice-Chancellor's Poetry Prizes, and awarded First Prize in the 2017 University of Canberra Health Poetry Prize, for his choral libretto, *And let the wonder in*. His poetry was included in Best Australian Poems 2015 & 2014 and he was winner of the 25th Launceston Poetry Cup (2010).

He composed and orchestrated the SATB oratorio, *Joan on Fire*, which was performed twice by the Melbourne Chamber Orchestra and Chorelation choir at the Melbourne Baptist Church. He was on the staff of the Australian Institute of Music, teaching Composition, Setting Poetry to Music, and Ensemble for two years.

He is more popularly known, internationally, for writing and performing the song, *Shaddap You Face* (1980-81) which was the Number One 45 rpm record (when they made 45 rpm records!) on the pop charts in a dozen countries and held the nine-times platinum award for the most successful song in Australian music history, for four decades. To date, *Shaddap You Face* has been translated into over 10 languages, including Papua New Guinea *pidgin* and the Western Australian aboriginal *Indjibundji* dialect.

He is co-writer, with his partner, Lin van Hek, of the song *Intimacy*, which was part of the soundtrack of the sci-fi masterpiece, *The Terminator*, selected as part of the United States Library of Congress National Film Registry archives.

His songs have been recorded, internationally, by scores of artists.

In 1981, he was presented with the Advance Australia Award by Sir Rupert James Hamer, AC, KCMG, ED, Premier of Victoria.